KT-513-471

HINDU

King's Road Primary School
Rosyth - Tel: 313470

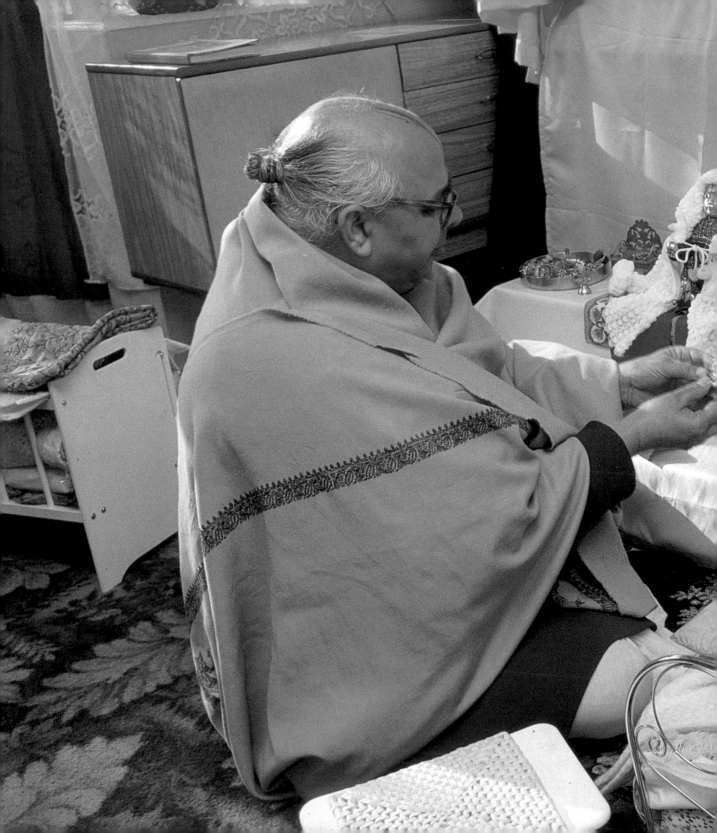

© 1988 Watts Books
Paperback edition 1995

This edition 1996

Watts Books
96 Leonard Street
London
EC2A 4RH

Franklin Watts Australia
14 Mars Road
Lane Cove
N.S.W. 2066

UK ISBN: 0 86313 672 9 (hardback)
UK ISBN: 0 7496 2268 7 (paperback)

Dewey Decimal Classification Number 294.5

Design: Edward Kinsey

Typesetting: Tradespools Ltd

Printed by G. Canale, Turin, Italy

The Publishers would like to thank
the Goswami family and all other
people shown in this book.

A.T.S. Ratna Singham is Chief Co-
ordinator of the Shri Ganapathy
Temple in Wimbledon, South
London

Note: Many of the photographs in
this book originally appeared in
'My Belief: I am a Hindu'

HINDU

Jenny Wood

Photographs: Chris Fairclough
Consultant: A.T.S. Ratna Singham

Watts Books
London/New York/Sydney

These people are Hindus.
They follow the Hindu religion
which began in India
thousands of years ago.

Hindus believe there is
one great God, called Brahman.
There are also many other gods
that look like animals or humans.

Many Hindus have altars
in their homes.
Some have special rooms
where statues of the gods are kept.

Most Hindu men wear European clothes.

Most Hindu women wear a long dress,
called a sari. Many also wear
a jewel in their nose, as well as
bracelets and other jewellery.

This man is a Hindu priest.
The special sign
on his forehead shows
that he worships the god Krishna.

Before every meal,
he offers food to the gods.
This makes the food holy.

Hindu children learn the teachings of the Holy Books.

The Hindu Holy Books are written in a special script called Sanskrit.

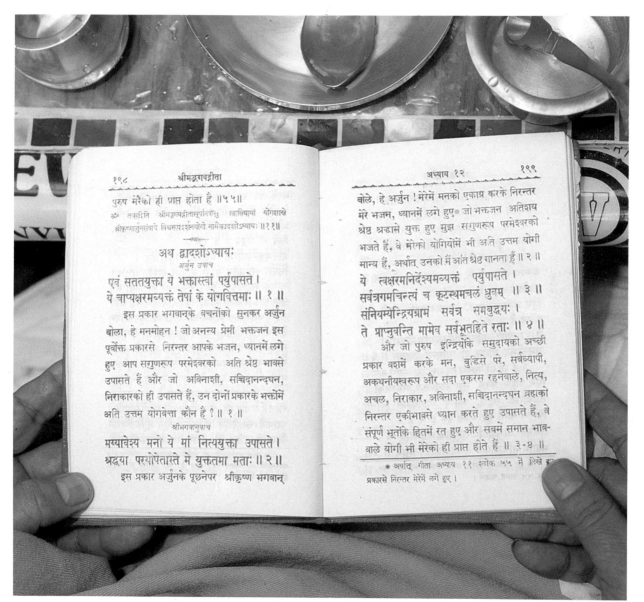

A Hindu temple is called a mandir.
Before going inside,
Hindus take off their shoes.
They say prayers
in front of a sacred flame.

The priest carries out
a special ceremony.
He moves a tray
with five candles
slowly in front of a god.

Most Hindus do not eat meat.
A favourite meal is vegetable curry
and a type of bread called puri.

Hindus have many rules about eating.
They must be clean
before they sit down for a meal.

A Hindu wedding ceremony
takes place in the temple,
under a special canopy.

The bride and groom take seven steps
around a sacred flame
to bless their marriage.
Their friends give them gifts
and wish them a happy life together.

After the ceremony, a meal is cooked in the temple kitchen.

Hindu festivals are happy occasions.
During Raksha Bandhan,
girls tie symbols called rakhis
on their brothers' wrists
in return for their protection.

Holi is the festival to celebrate
the start of spring.
Hindu children throw coloured powder
and water at each other.

Diwali is the festival of light.
There are firework displays,
and homes are lit
by lamps, candles and sparklers.

At the end of every day,
a Hindu family comes together
to pray and sing hymns.

FACTS ABOUT HINDUS

Hinduism is one of the oldest religions in the world. It began in India over 4,000 years ago.

Hindus believe that:
– the spirit of God is present in everything in the world – animals, plants and humans
– it is wrong to hurt any living thing
– a person has many lives and is reborn after death
– the way a person behaves during a lifetime will decide what their next life will be like
– a person has duties to their family and to God.

Hinduism divides people into social groups or castes.

Hinduism is the third largest religion in the world with over 500 million followers.

Most Hindus live in India, but they are also found in other parts of the world such as East Africa, Sri Lanka, Europe and North America.

In Britain there are about 300,000 Hindus. They came from East Africa, India and Pakistan.

GLOSSARY

Altar
A table or platform used for religious ceremonies.

Brahman
The Hindu word for God.

Diwali
The Hindu festival of light.

Holi
The Hindu festival which celebrates the start of spring.

Krishna
A Hindu god.

Mandir
A Hindu temple.

Raksha Bandhan
During this festival, a Hindu girl ties a symbol called a rakhi on a brother's wrist in return for his protection.

Sanskrit
The special script in which the Hindu Holy Books are written.

Sari
The traditional dress of Hindu women, made from one piece of cloth wound round the body.

INDEX

Altar 9

Brahman 8, 28

Ceremony 17, 20, 22, 28
Clothes 10

Diwali 25, 28

Festival 23, 24, 25, 28
Food 13

God(s) 8, 9, 12, 13 17, 27, 28

Holi 24, 28
Holy Books 14, 15, 28

India 7, 27

Krishna 12, 28

Mandir 16, 28

Prayers 16
Priest 12, 17
Puri 18

Rakhi 23, 28
Raksha Bandhan 23, 28

Sanskrit 15, 28
Sari 11, 28
Statues 9

Temple 16, 20, 22, 28

Wedding 20

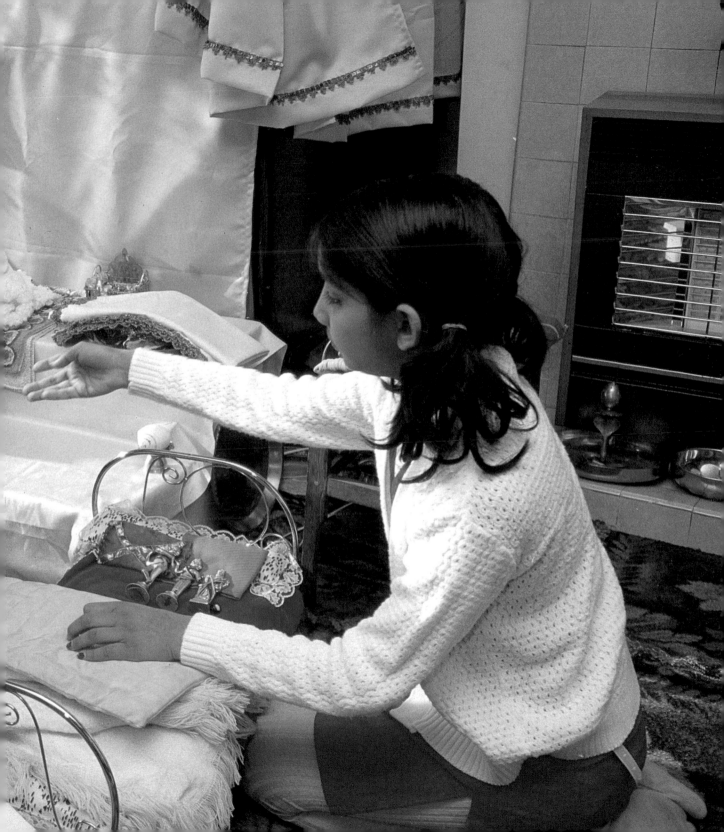

King's Road Primary School
Rosyth - Tel: 313470

KT-430-367

C333251953

For: Maisey

Rockpool Children's Books
15 North Street
Marton
Warwickshire
CV23 9RJ

First published in Great Britain by Rockpool Children's Books Ltd. 2012
Text and Illustrations copyright © Sam Walshaw 2011
Sam Walshaw has asserted the moral rights
to be identified as the author and illustrator of this book.

A CIP catalogue record of this book is available
from the British Library.
All rights reserved

Printed in China

rockpool
children's books

Sam Walshaw

Maisey and the Pirates

The Sea Monster

One day, Captain Codeye found
an old treasure map.
"Aha!" he said, "X marks the spot
where the sunken treasure is."

"It's a pirate's job to find hidden treasure,"
he told his pirate crew on the good ship Barnacle.
"We're all setting sail for X marks the spot."

Soon Captain Codeye spied the X down below.
"Drop the anchor, Crazy Maisey," he yelled.
"We'll have to dive to the bottom of the sea
to get to that sunken treasure."

"Aye-aye, Captain!" Maisey replied.

"Take a deep breath," gasped Cra...

SPLASH!

Captain Codeye
and Crazy Maisey
jumped in and swam
straight down to the seabed.

"There's the treasure,"
gurgled Crazy Maisey.

"Fill your boots," bubbled Captain Codeye.
"Now let's head back up."

Crazy Maisey and
Captain Codeye swam up
towards the trusty Barnacle.
They couldn't wait to show the
treasure to the others, but just
as they were nearly there...

...they spotted a great big purple, popeyed, pirate-eating sea monster heading their way – and he looked very grumpy.

"Oh no –
It's the purple, popeyed,
pirate-eating sea monster,"
gasped Captain Codeye. **"QUICK!"**

Captain Codeye and Crazy Maisey
leapt up out of the sea and landed safely
on the deck of the Barnacle.

"Hoist the sails,"
ordered Captain Codeye.
"It's the purple, popeyed,
pirate-eating sea monster!"

Daisy jumped to work and hoisted the sails.

Suddenly, the purple, popeyed, pirate-eating
sea monster popped up out of the sea
and snarled at them, "Rooaaarrr!"

At first,
they were all too scared to do anything.
But then Daisy took charge – even though
she was the smallest pirate.

She stomped right up to the monster and told him
off for being such a mean, grumpy bully.

The purple, popeyed, pirate-
eating sea monster was so
shocked he burst into tears.

"Oh, there, there," said Daisy.
She gave the monster a hug and
a tissue and invited him on to
the Barnacle for buns and cakes –
as long as he behaved himself.

The monster was shy at first...

...but he felt better when he had
a piece of cake, and the pirates saw
he really was quite a nice monster after all.

The monster said he was sorry for being so mean and grumpy. "I've got this terrible itch on my back. It's made me meaner and meaner, and grumpier and grumpier," he explained.

Daisy had a look.
"Blistering barnacles!" she squeaked.
"There's an octopus stuck down your pants.
His tentacles must have been tickling
you all this time. I'll pull him out."

"Aaaahhh..."
At last the itch had gone.

The monster felt so much better, he promised not to scare anyone again – at least not on purpose.

"By the way," he said, "I don't really eat pirates. I'd much rather have a nice currant bun."

The monster thanked the crew
of the good ship Barnacle
and went on his way. He was a
much happier monster now that
he'd got rid of that itch...

...and the octopus was pleased
to be out of his pants too!